When I Wasn't Looking

When I Wasn't Looking

Poems by
Victoria Sullivan

Art and Design by
Barbara Milman

Red Parrot Press

Published 2012
by Red Parrot Press
www.redparrotpress.com

ISBN-13: 978-0972173162
ISBN-10: 0972173161

for Natasha & Sabina

for Daniel Rancour-Laferriere

THE TRANSFORMATION

A green tree guards the end of my meadow,
bushy green needles showing up its brown
neighbors—those bare trees, those skeletons.
I want to be like the green tree, lush and
comforting. I want to turn my arms into branches,
my flesh into scented needles. I want to live
on sunshine and rain, driving my hungry roots
down, down into the dark earth, holding all the pain
of the world and converting it to lovely vegetation.

I want to be the tree that blesses the meadow,
wooing the warm wind that caresses the deer,
who wander shyly into the meadow and even
the crows—whom I do not particularly love—
will be allowed to peck at the paltry grasses
in my vicinity. I suppose the crows have some function.
They do, of course, gobble up road-kill.

So, yes, even the crows can come to dine
in my meadow when I am a tree, when I cease
to be human, when I join the seasons,
naked out of doors, a tree in the universe,
destined to live for many decades,
destined to give shade to those I've never met,
even to those not yet born. When I am a tree,
I will be kind at last to every creature.
When I am a tree, I will finally know
the deep joy of selfless love.

WINTER DAYS, WINTER NIGHTS

I have fallen in love with winter.
Its honesty. With the trees bare,
nothing is hidden. Like a middle-aged
woman standing naked in front of a mirror.
It takes guts. This winter so far
is pale, crisp, cold, lonely.

But the pale grays and blues, the slightly
anemic sun, they give a kind of pure,
raw life experience… as if we lived
long ago, in a simpler if crueler time.

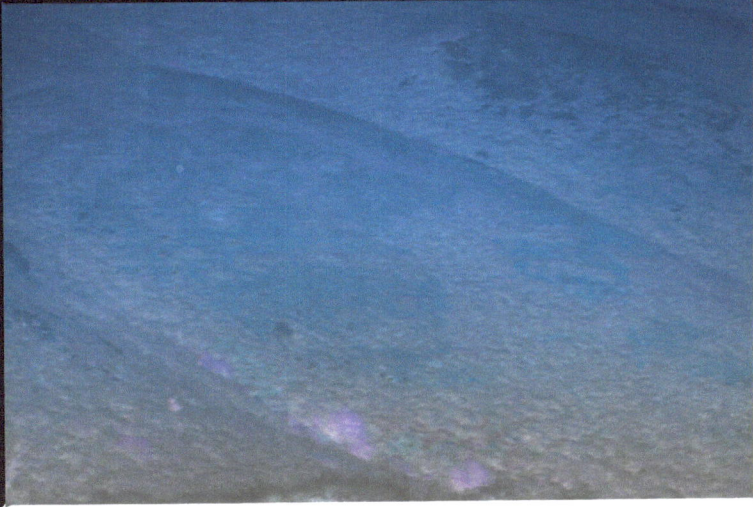

Like the bears, we're probably meant
to hibernate…or at the least, spend
more time in bed. It's quiet outside.

I have fallen in love with winter,
and I hope that doesn't mean
I'm craving death… or the winter of
my body…so unloved now. It's hard to say.
When you fall in love with winter
you don't expect passion any more…
just the pale sky and the weak sun,
and maybe a laugh or two…
something to get you through.
You are a winter lover now.
You can't ask too much.

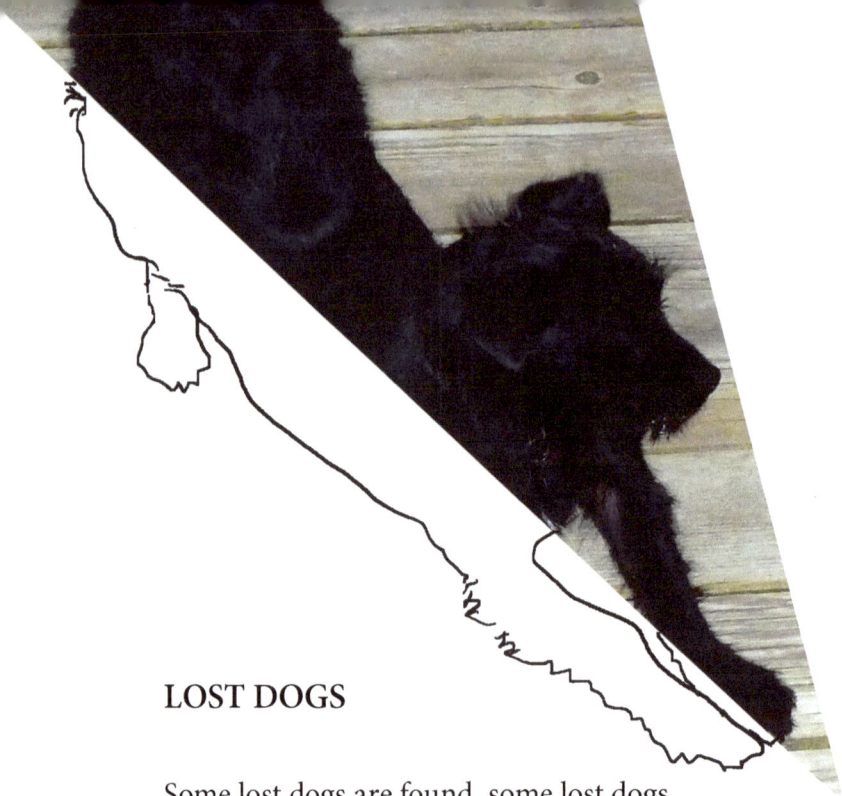

LOST DOGS

Some lost dogs are found, some lost dogs
are not. So when I see the signs posted on
electric poles — he's brown and black —
I have to wonder if this particular dog
will be found or not. And my lover,
I like to call him that, it's probably
an overstatement, my lover has to put down
his cat; he's riddled with cancer. The cat,
not my lover, who would fall more easily
into that category if he called me more often.
Or at all. But what's a lover anyway?
Something like a lost dog, I suspect,
wandering the countryside, sniffing, a little hungry,
a little full. When he's in the mood,
he's in the mood. But it might take a couple
of shots of tequila to put him there.

RENTING A FARMER
— for Doug —

I heard it on the radio:
You can rent a farmer.
But for what, they didn't say,
and I'm kind of wondering if
you can rent them for something
other than farming? Say, like
putting up your storm windows,
or gathering leaves, or,
well, say, something more
intimate maybe. Would a farmer
be rentable for building a fire,
and then shaking the martinis,
and next sitting down on the couch
with the lady of the house
at dusk, the sky a pale magenta?
And while some jazz plays on the radio,
could she and the farmer
maybe get better acquainted?
And if so, whom does one call
to rent these willing farmers?

AFTER & AFTER & AFTER

It's always after something: after you left school,
or after you married or had the baby or divorced,
or your lover died, or you lost the house,
or you were no longer young. It's always
after something in your life. But the humorous part is
that the after part is just like the before part, it's another
new part, a phase we used to call it. He's in a phase
we would say to our friend with the hyper-cranky fifteen year old son
or the husband who was suddenly wearing an earring or
the period when you can't write and you think you'll never
write again. It's just a phase we would say.

But everything is a phase, it seems, and one follows another
helter-skelter, like daffodils in spring, or rain after the first low
distant rumbles of thunder. And as phases go, the ones
that come next always surprise us. Never thought I'd be
this crazy still at my age, I say, and you look at me with
big doubting eyes. Really? You ask in your cynical tone.
I could have told you you'd be out of control forever.

Thank you, thank you for that blessing, I say. Now
I can sleep peacefully because I know I will never
truly settle down. Just take a break once in a while.
And then it's off on one more bizarre life adventure:
walking down the pitted dirt road in the dark,
without a flash light of course, beside the dense forest
into another after phase, and only slightly drunk.

IN THE LITTLE HOUSE
— March 2009 —

The snow melts so slowly from my small meadow,
it makes me think of the ice age,
the terminal moraine that lasted
thousands of years.   Maybe more.
Past time is so complex. It's mostly
a guess, I suspect, like the economic crisis,
where we don't know just how much these banks
will bleed, and where to place the tourniquet,
and how to print so many billions of bills,
the presses running night and day, coughing out
bogus cash for these running dogs, these bankers.

But never mind them. It's the snow and the ice
that command my attention, the long slow overly cold winter,
the people I know who fell on ice and broke their wrists
or ribs, more than usual I think. And then the sums of money
I've been bleeding for oil so my house doesn't freeze
and I can manage to walk around without my bones
shaking from the cold. It's one of those winters: Mean.

And now I've lost my lover on top of all that:
on top of the ice, and the falling market,
and the energy bills, I've lost my lover.
So the question arises whether I should give it all up
and become an alcoholic, or maybe study Sanskrit,
or keep on eating junk food and hiding
under my electric blanket...
waiting for deliverance of some sort.
I don't want to be caught howling at the moon.
There's such a thing as emotional decorum,
and I am, if all goes well, intending to embody it.

THE COMING

When you see the brown leafless trees in March,
and some of them are gone, the spaces where
the trees were, but they died and fell over in the storms,
and the absent trees are present in their absence,
like your beloved who died and left a great gaping
space in your heart, a dark parched place
as if a fire storm had blown something essential
away, and you mourn for the absent trees
and for your beloved who comes to you now
only in dreams. This is what nature is:
the presence and the absence,
the leafless tree with its stiff brown twigs,
and the lover who died in the full blown
thrust of his manhood, not old and grey,
but still vigorous until he wasn't.
These things are part of life. Death is part of life,
and yet we run and hide and declare
ourselves invulnerable. But nature knows
the story is always death and renewal,

the winter and the spring. Whether we live
long or short, we all, like the leaves and trees,
will one day blast off into who knows
what distant journey. If you look at the stars at night,
if you toss your head back and gaze up at their light,
what you see is already something other.

The light has been traveling towards you for thousands
of years, waiting to shine on just this black night,
on you, standing in your driveway looking up in wonder.

THE DEER'S WORLD

The deer must like the snow.
In this latest March blizzard
they arrive in masses —
first at twilight on the road, three
of them, arranged like an odd
painting: two facing each other,
nose to nose, and one, smaller, watching,
a family scene, dead in the middle of
Glasco Turnpike, like it wasn't a road.
But then, the snow drifted and unplowed,
it wasn't a road, although I drove it.
They stared at me as if I were an alien
intruder in my big slow metal vehicle.

At home, below in my small meadow
in the dusk, many deer, eight, ten, twelve —
I couldn't count as I drove up the little hill,
praying the snow tires would do their work
and get me home. The deer were happy
and serene. The snow had returned
their turf to an undifferentiated landscape,
more theirs than ours in its perfect whiteness.

Now awake the next day, my car buried in the blizzard,
I wish I had stopped on the road and let the deer
kiss — or whatever they were doing — for eternity.

IT GOT DARK

It got dark when I wasn't looking.
Suddenly it is dead black outside,
and the floor feels colder through my sox,
and the only way I can survive this season
is to have an electric blanket.

It got dark when I wasn't looking
and suddenly my sister's mind is gone,
shot full of holes, and confusions like
strange growths upon the purity of her
neuron connections. She knows me,
but she doesn't know the name of where
she lives or why she just sits and sits all day.

It got dark when I wasn't looking
and all the politicians turned into raving
lunatics, except for the quiet ones
that just steal your money and smile and smile.
Like Hamlet said, you can smile and smile
and be a villain. I swear I vote every year,
so I actually was looking, but it happened anyway.

It got dark when I wasn't looking,
and someone fatally shot the book industry
along with the record industry, and theatre
became simply entertainment, and art became
a dead stuffed horse hanging from the ceiling.
And athletes all take steroids and won't play for
anything under ten million dollars a season.
And the jazz clubs have disappeared.

It got dark when I wasn't looking. It got real dark.

MOURNING SONG

— for Steve —

I was singing in an old willow tree,
I was singing, that bird was me.
I was singing and the branches swooned,
down to the ground and rustled there.
I was singing a song of love
for the fellows who died
and were buried around.
I was wearing a fetching gown.
Did you hear me singing in the old willow tree?
Did you hear my heart bursting
and know it was me?
He's under the ground, my true love,
and I will be singing for eternity.

LATE MAY IN APOCALYPTIC TIMES

I woke up to a butter gold room. It was time for sun
after ten days of rain. In the mid-west, tornadoes
were leaving whole towns and cities flat. So this is
the extreme weather we've been promised.   But no
way to grasp how long it will last…and at least the Rapture
didn't arrive, just the usual volcanic eruptions in Iceland,
and randy old French men jumping maids in posh hotels.
Business as usual, except for the weather. The benefit of
the rain is that everything is green, shades of green,
green leaves dragging down tall green trees. And now that the sun
is back, I once more understand the ancient worship
of the sun god. What could be better than this butter gold bliss?

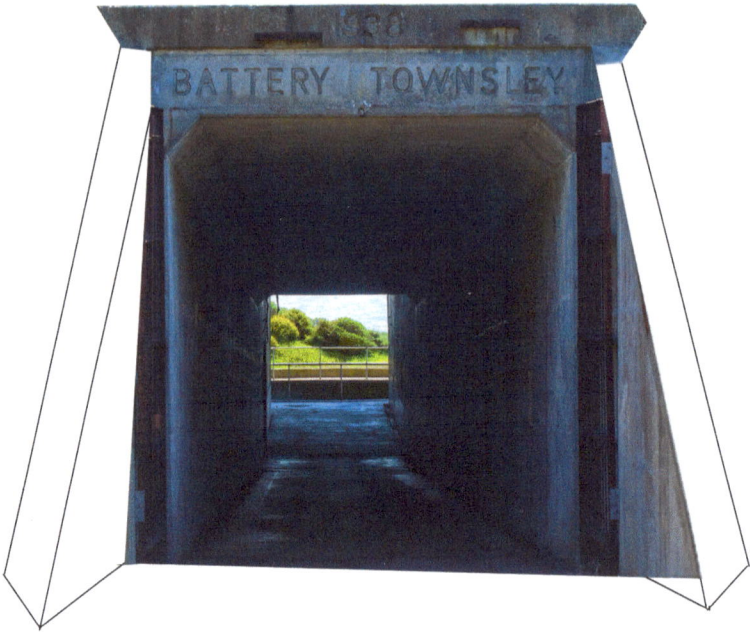

AH YES, IT COULD ALMOST BE SPRING

The air is chill and spring refuses to take hold,
like a recalcitrant adolescent lying late in bed
and avoiding the day. The air is nasty.
Even the skin on my back is cold. Is this
what it's like to grow old? No wonder the old
wear so many sweaters, and they like to complain.
But I am the same. It's a good thing my furnace
works, and the few bright daffodils outside
are holding their own in the bitter air.

We make ourselves into little worlds and wait
for deliverance — like lonely travelers
on a long dark road. The business of life
is not easy. This is when you really want another
by your side, someone to crack a joke
or give a hug, someone to find you amusing
or sexy or just plain there. A companion.

But if no one arrives, then it's best to strive
to keep a little grin on your face, drink hot tea,
read a book. The spring can't wait forever.
It will come, and — oh joy — you can always
put another blanket on the bed.

The thing about life is, it has a way of changing:
now up, now down, now rich, now poor,
now to be envied, now to be pitied. So the best
approach is to turn Buddhist. Then everything
is as it should be. Drop the attachments.
Look at the stars, Give away all you own.
Take to the road. Well, perhaps that's getting
carried away. Maybe a hot bath is all I need
and the dream of a lover, the satisfaction of
a blissful fantasy. Because, I am told,
some folks even refuse to fantasize.
But not me. I live in that realm, and plan
to continue until one day the flesh falls away,
freeing my soul to soar into another atmosphere:
part tree, part soil, part wood thrush
singing rebirth in every breath,
singing rebirth for all the other
yearning souls. Amen, the small bird
cries, Amen and Hallelujah.

LITTLE DOSES

Give me love. Give me love in little doses,
give me love. I am ready for your fingers
on my forehead where a stray hair needs
adjustment, and don't forget to touch my neck,
and kiss my cheek, and rub those places on my back
where my body cries out for your hands. Give me
love, and I'll return it multiplied for your pleasure.
First, just step into my door, when the day is over,
and you're sorely tired from the petty business of our lives.
You will stand there looking gritty, I will move to embrace
you, hug you tight, and sniff your neck, reacquaint myself
with who you are, the way you want to hear a little music,
read the paper, drink a beer. There's no rush. I understand.

I will make a little dinner, I will tell you my day's tales.
We can laugh and be irreverent, we can settle in.
Give me love in little doses. I don't ask for anything more.
Just don't stop it coming, baby. I am hungry for your presence,
I am waiting here for you. Put a smile on your face, and
I'll put one on for you. Give me love. I long to taste you,
and lie down by your side. Give me love in little doses
and I'll love you far and wide. You're the one for me,
 you know, and life is drifting swiftly on. So give me love.
just here, just now, give me love before I die.

IN THE FUTURE

A crow flies low over the fields,
black wings of death, searching
for carrion. The land delivers:
earth harsh and baked and poisoned
by hydraulic drilling. No crops thriving.
Here where we used to walk with joy
among the fields of gold, here now,
barren like a sick womb, victim
of foolish greed. We cannot drink
the water, and leafless apple trees
are dying from the roots up. Folks have
strange goiters, allergies, trouble breathing.
And did you see it? the water gushing up
from the wells: brown bubbling sludge.

Perhaps you knew this place once upon a time
back in the day? They say the Hudson
Valley was a lovely spot, and that folks
traveled here for the clean air of the Catskills,
surrounded by fertile fields and water so sweet
and pure, it needed no filter. That was back
before the fracking began. Oh yes, I remember...

Now only the crows glow with radiant health,
their harsh cries the only music in the skies.
Lords of death, they blaze across the bruised land,
triumphant mascots of natural gas drilling,
victors in a battle that has left the earth in tears.

THE TERRORS OF TRAVEL

On the runway going nowhere — that's the worst.
You're due to take off, but haven't.
Or you've actually arrived but somehow
cannot get to the unloading dock.
Stuck, like in your nightmares,
arrival or departure delayed. You're in the plane
but on the ground; it grows stuffy in the economy cabin.

And of course you have a connecting flight to make,
and it's tight and requires running full speed
through the strange airport in the crowded city,
and you'd like to stop and pee, but have no time.
And yet actually you are going nowhere, and the minutes
are ticking by, and those around you are growing
increasingly cranky. There's this woman next to you
who wants you to join her in her rage. *How dare they
make us just sit here? How dare they?!*

Can you make it? Will you? No way to know.
Air gone stale, the captain's voice sounds
tired as he makes the meaningless excuses.

Like every crisis in your life, this one too is shrouded
in mystery. You could miss the plane, or the perfect lover,
or the great promotion. These things hang by a thread.
You could be sitting on that next flight beside the only person
you'd ever really love and who' d love you too. Deeply.
But you're strangers now and damned if you don't miss
the connection. And so all bets are off.

GODDESS SONG

They're holding a goddess festival in town
and of course I'm thinking of going.
I've climbed down from the moon, donned
human clothes, brushed my teeth,
combed my mane, and am searching for
stray stars to hang about my throat—
flashing lights to call you home.

Home is what I call my body when
you're around. Home is the goddess nest,
the spice bush, home is where I entice you in
to the sound of gentle wind chimes
while the sweet port in my mouth
dribbles from my lips into yours.

Listen, love, to the wind in the leaves,
listen to my heart beating its song.

I am being called to the goddess festival.
I've climbed down from the moon where
it's cold and lonely. I'm abandoning
Diana's bow. Just hold out your arms.
Home is what I call my body and your body.
Listen to my heart beating for you.
They say human men make lovely consorts
and I do adore the smell of your hair.

DAYS OF RAIN

When you have days and days of rain, and you live
surrounded by trees and green, you feel the power.
The relentless drumming on the thirsty earth,
the strange half whispery sound. And as the days
pass, the rain continues, bringing mid-day times
of darkness, a grayness that is deep and somber.
But all the time the green is growing stronger,
and all around the little cabin a wilderness presides.

It is good for the soul of the city person to be in all
this wet long drink of nature, this thirst that goes
on and on being satisfied, this pouring of tears
from the skies, amid distant rumbles of thunder.

It's the best weather to get that phone call from your lover
who's tired of being wet, working outside, and needs
some comfort. There goes your writing project.
Here he comes in his jeans and his hard on.
Here he comes with his crooked grin and his body hunger.
So you slip from your clothes and give thanks to the rain.

SUMMER BLISS

Birds are quiet in their flight. It's their chirping
not their flying that we note. Only lying in the hammock,
still under the tall trees do I observe just how many birds
are flying about, quietly, softly landing, tree to tree,
and dipping through the air like feathered darts.

And all this rich life is there and goes unnoted
unless I am lying in the hammock, and the day
is still. What else goes unnoted?
Whose smiles, whose tears?   All the little tragedies
and triumphs of people swarming around me.

What about the handsome dark-eyed man
who was on heroin for 27 years, and now is not,
but he can't write poetry any more. That door
has closed. He says his life is quieter. He's on Zoloft
for the depression. His mild smile greets my poems.

He's happy he wrote many notebooks full, once,
but that was, as he says, "under the influence."
Now he is sober and quiet. Now the poetry is gone.
And some days, when I'm not in the hammock,
I think the birds are gone too. But really they are flying
quietly above me in the tops of trees. So what we think
we see and know is sometimes hidden like a heroin dream,
gone to our eyes but not our souls, here but invisible —
like the sweetest wisps of childhood memories:
those vast summer nights when the twilight was endless.

NIGHT AND THE SOUL

— for Jane and Nicola —

Night gently falling in the tropics, the sky a serene
grey now, with black palms framed against it.
Dark night like the secret puma approaching,
and in Haiti the dead are buried under so many
tons of ruble that their crushed bodies will never
be whole again. So we must simply bless their souls.

It is hard to view the suffering of the innocent,
but to be blind to this is worse still.
We know that all who are born will one day die.
It is nature's way, and we are part of nature.

The tides roll in, the moon climbs the sky.
We do not control the universe, no matter
our deep desire to land on Mars or colonize the moon.

We are the children of darkness, unless we let
our souls discover light. We are the laughter
in the trees, the wild white heron landing on the shore.
We are more than our bodies. We need to bless
the Haitians and ourselves. We need to bless
all sentient creatures, and then lie down to sleep
the sleep of innocence, the sleep that heals
the wounds of those who suffer and those who
impose suffering. We are simply animals
who might be wise, if we work on it,
and fools if we willingly buy the pap
the powerful wish to purvey in our direction.

Alone we stumble in the dark. Together
we rise like living hearts into the brilliant skies.

ZEN

Every day is a good day
if you are prepared
to meet it.
Stillness helps.
So do sleep and dreams.
The large lovely room
in the dream,
like a cathedral,
filled with art and plants,
is your own spirit
magnified. Go to the room
and breathe the air.

Fear nothing.

This is the journey
to the deep self.
Breathing will lead
you there.

Never despair.

Those dark clouds
in your mind
are filled with fruitful rain.
Lie down on the earth
and be reborn.
Every day is a good day.

Poet and playwright Victoria Sullivan has performed her poetry in a variety of venues from New York City and the Hudson Valley to Cairo, Egypt, as well as on radio and television. Her three prior chapbooks are EATING FIGS AT TWILIGHT, ALZHEIMER DREAMS and THE DIVIDED BED. Her poetry has appeared in numerous journals. Sullivan is also "Poet Laureate of the Woodstock Roundtable" on WDST Radio 100.1. She resides in both Saugerties, NY and New York City.

Barbara Milman is a book artist and printmaker living in the San Francisco Bay Area. Her work has been exhibited throughout the United States. Her hand-made artist books can be found in the special collections of many museums, university libraries and public libraries. Her previously published books include LIGHT IN THE SHADOWS, ZOE'S JOURNAL and ALZHEIMER DREAMS. She is past president of the California Society of Printmakers.